Chocolate

Saviour Pirotta

an imprint of Hodder Children's Books

Text copyright © Saviour Pirotta 2003

Consultant: Carol Ballard
Language consultant: Andrew Burrell
Design: Perry Tate Design

Published in Great Britain in 2003
by Hodder Wayland, an imprint of
Hodder Children's Books

The publishers would like to thank the following for allowing us to reproduce their
pictures in this book: Anthony Blake Library; cover, title page, contents page, 4
Maximilian Stock, 6 (bottom) Joff Lee, 8 Graham Salter, 13, 14, 17 Tim Hill, 20 John
Sims, 22 Maximilian Stock, 23 (left), 24, (top and fourth from top) / Cephas; 5, 9, 10
(top), 11, 12, 19, 24 (bottom) / Corbis; 6 (top) Jennie Woodcock Reflections
Photolibrary, 7 Richard Gross Photography, 10 (bottom) Buddy Mays, 16 Owen
Franken, 23, 24 (second and third from top) / Dorling Kindersley Images; 15 /
Cadburys; 18 / Food Features; 21

A Catalogue record for this book is available from the British Library.

ISBN: 0750244232

Printed and bound in Singapore

Hodder Children's Books
A division of Hodder Headline Limited
338 Euston Road, London NW1 3BH

Contents

Yummy chocolate

Chocolate is delicious! Dark chocolate, milk chocolate, white chocolate.

Chocolate comes in all shapes and sizes. You can buy chocolate bars, chocolate eggs, chocolate biscuits and even chocolate buttons.
Yum! Yum!

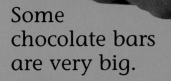

Some
chocolate bars
are very big.

Chocolate
chips are
very small.

5

There are many ways to enjoy chocolate. Chew it. Drink it. Lick it off your sticky fingers!

Chocolate cake is soft and gooey.

Nothing warms you up like a cup of hot chocolate when it's cold. Nothing cools you down like chocolate ice cream when it's hot.

Chocolate ice cream melts in your mouth.

Chocolate trees

Chocolate is made from the beans of cacao trees. The trees grow in hot countries, where it also rains a lot.

HUGE pods grOW on the cacao trees, either on the branches or on the trunk itself.

8

Inside the pods, is a sticky pulp. And, hidden in the pulp, are lots of beans. They are called cocoa beans.

A pod can have as many as 50 beans inside it. That's enough to make more chocolate than you can eat in one go!

Get those pods

When the pods are ripe, the farmers cut them down. They use large hooks on poles to reach the ones at the top.

The pods turn orange or red when they're ready to be picked.

The farmers crack
the pods open
with their knives.
They scoop out
the pulp with the
beans inside it.

Piles of pulp and beans are left outdoors for
a few days. The heat from the sun turns the
beans deep brown and gives them a nice
chocolate flavour.

When the beans turn a rich, chocolate brown, they are picked out of the pulp.

The farmers **spread** them out on mats, tables and the flat roofs of their houses to dry in the sun.

Cocoa beans need a lot of warmth to dry.

At last the beans are perfectly dry. They are packed in sacks and sent to chocolate factories all over the world.

These beans are ready to be turned into chocolate.

The chocolate factory

At the chocolate factory, the beans are cleaned, to make sure there is no dirt left on them. Then they are roasted in huge, hot ovens. This makes them smell of chocolate.

These beans have been roasted and are now cooling down.

Next the shells are cracked open so that only the insides are left.

The insides of the beans are called 'nibs'.

nib

shell

The nibs are ground into a thick, dark paste called 'cocoa mass'. Then the paste is SQUEEZED until cocoa butter and cocoa powder come out of it.

Cocoa butter makes chocolate melt in your mouth.

Cocoa powder can be used to make chocolate drinks and flavour cakes.

Making Chocolate

The chocolate makers put cocoa mass in a GIANT mixing machine. They add cocoa butter, milk and sugar.

Round and round goes the mixer, until all the ingredients are mixed together.

Steel rollers
then crush the
mixture until
it's nice and
smooth.

Making chocolate
takes a long, long
time.

19

At last the chocolate makers taste the chocolate. Hmmm, it tastes just right. It's time to pour it into moulds and wait until it sets.

The warm chocolate will soon set.

Soon the chocolate will be in the shops, ready for you to buy.

Chocolate is one of the most popular foods in the world.

Choccy chocolate!

You can buy Easter eggs for Easter. Chocolate Santas for Christmas. Heart shaped chocolates for St. Valentine's Day.

Chocolate helps us celebrate. Yum! Yum!

Glossary and index